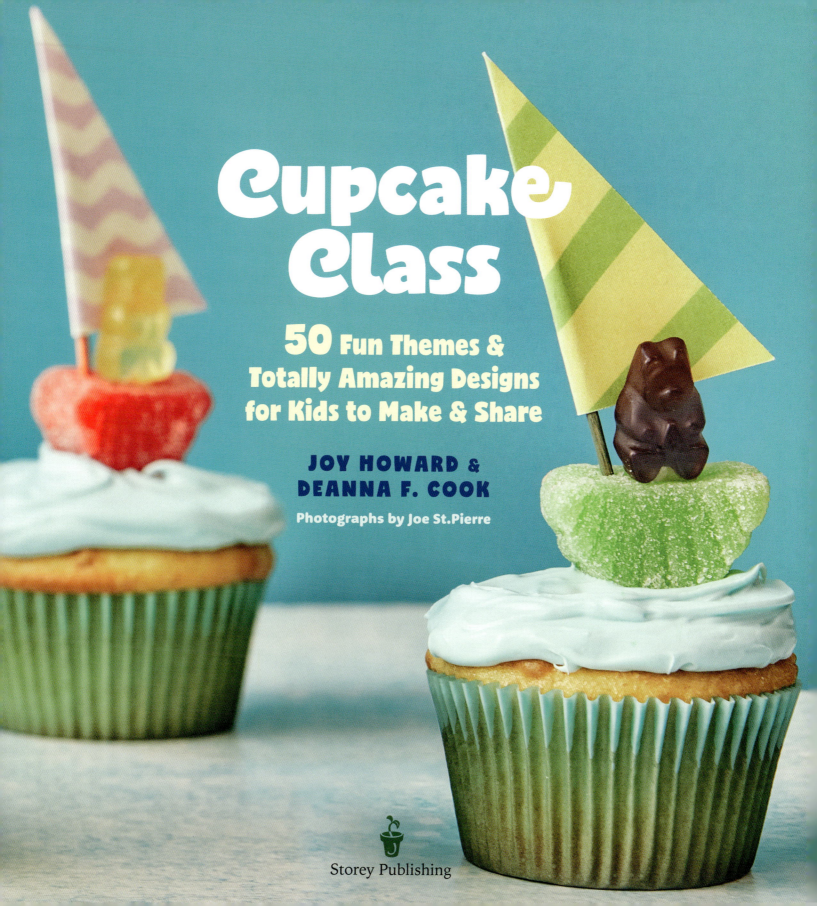

*The mission of Storey Publishing is to serve our customers by publishing practical information that encourages personal independence in harmony with the environment.*

**Edited by** Lisa H. Hiley
**Art direction and book design by** Carolyn Eckert
**Text production by** Jennifer Jepson Smith

**Cover and interior photography by** © Joe St.Pierre
**Photo styling by** Joy Howard
**Illustrations by** © Clare Owen, 13, 142, 147–156
**Additional illustrations by** Alyssa Ly © Storey Publishing, cover and interior doodles and line art (throughout); © Emily Balsley, 1 and throughout, 10, 11, 38, 47 and throughout (bird and butterfly), 54 and throughout (stars), 91 b. and throughout, 96 ladybug; © Vector Jura/Shutterstock.com, cover (title lettering background)

Text © 2025 by Joy Howard and Deanna F. Cook

All rights reserved. Hachette Book Group supports the right to free expression and the value of copyright. The purpose of copyright is to encourage writers and artists to produce the creative works that enrich our culture. The scanning, uploading, and distribution of this book without permission is a theft of the authors' intellectual property. If you would like permission to use material from the book (other than for review purposes), please contact permissions@hbgusa.com. Thank you for your support of the authors' rights.

The information in this book is true and complete to the best of our knowledge. All recommendations are made without guarantee on the part of the authors or Storey Publishing. The authors and publisher disclaim any liability in connection with the use of this information.

The publisher is not responsible for websites (or their content) that are not owned by the publisher.

Storey books may be purchased in bulk for business, educational, or promotional use. Special editions or book excerpts can also be created to specification. For details, please contact your local bookseller or the Hachette Book Group Special Markets Department at special.markets @hbgusa.com.

**Storey Publishing**
210 MASS MoCA Way
North Adams, MA 01247
storey.com

Storey Publishing is an imprint of Workman Publishing, a division of Hachette Book Group, Inc., 1290 Avenue of the Americas, New York, NY 10104. The Storey Publishing name and logo are registered trademarks of Hachette Book Group, Inc.

Distributed in Europe by Hachette Livre, 58 rue Jean Bleuzen, 92 178 Vanves Cedex, France
Distributed in the United Kingdom by Hachette UK Ltd., Carmelite House, 50 Victoria Embankment, London EC4Y 0DZ

ISBNs: 978-1-63586-852-4 (paper over board with 3 sticker sheets and 3 cardstock sheets); 978-1-63586-853-1 (ebook)

Printed in Humen Town, Dongguan, China by R. R. Donnelley on paper from responsible sources
10 9 8 7 6 5 4 3 2 1

APS 04/25

Library of Congress Cataloging-in-Publication Data on file

**For Zadie, Inez, Andiyah, Ella & Maisie**

who inspired many birthday cupcakes through the years!

YUM!

# Contents

**1** Welcome to Cupcake Class 8

**2** Develop Your Decorating Skills 22

**3** Sprinkles, Dots & Squiggles 36

**4** Animals, Animals Everywhere! 50

**5** Sea & Stars 68

**6** Nature Magic 92

**7** Funny Faces 110

**8** Let's Celebrate! 122

Index 140
Cupcake Extras 142

**Who doesn't love cupcakes?** They're more fun to eat than a slice of cake and can be decorated just about any way you can imagine. This book introduces you to the basics of baking cupcakes and making frosting, then teaches you dozens of cool techniques for making delicious works of art for your family and friends. Here are some ways to make the most of your treats.

**GIVE THE GIFT OF CUPCAKES.** Share some sweetness by making special cupcakes for parents, siblings, or friends to celebrate any occasion or none at all. You could bring your whole class cupcakes to celebrate a holiday or your teacher's birthday. Just make sure that your school allows homemade treats and no one in your class has food allergies.

**MAKE HOLIDAY CUPCAKES.** Bake up some holiday fun throughout the year. Make hearts for Valentine's Day (page 132), trees for Christmas (page 138), or Pumpkin Patch cupcakes for Halloween (page 136).

**HOST A CUPCAKE DECORATING PARTY!** Send out invitations (use the ones at the back of the book or make your own). Bake a couple of batches of cupcakes, set out colored frosting, candy, and sprinkles, and challenge friends to design edible masterpieces. At the end of the party, arrange the cupcakes on a table so everyone can ooh and aah before digging in. For favors, send guests home with wooden spoons and aprons, decorated at the party.

**HAVE A CUPCAKE BAKE SALE FOR A GOOD CAUSE.** Sell frosted cupcakes at a bake sale for $1 each. You can also set up a cupcake decorating tray with candies and sprinkles kids can add to their frosted cupcakes. Donate the proceeds to your school, sports team, local animal shelter, or another cause you support.

# A Few Baking Basics

If you want to be a cupcake pro, start by following these basic kitchen rules. Ask a grown-up for permission before using the kitchen and get their help as you need it along the way.

**1. WASH YOUR HANDS** with warm water and soap before you start baking or decorating.

**2. ROLL UP LONG SLEEVES** and wear an apron. Tie back long hair to keep it away from sticky frosting and batter. You can even wear a bandanna or chef's hat!

**3. READ THE DIRECTIONS** for baking and decorating from start to finish before you begin.

**4. GATHER** the required ingredients and tools before you start to be sure you have everything.

**5. MEASURE INGREDIENTS** carefully when baking your cupcakes, whether you use a cake mix or make them from scratch (see pages 16 and 18 for recipes).

**6. FOR BEST RESULTS,** line muffin tins with paper or silicone cups. Use an ice cream scoop or measuring cup to fill your muffin tins with batter. It's less messy than using a spoon, and the cupcakes will come out evenly sized.

**7. LET YOUR CUPCAKES COOL** completely on a rack before frosting them.

**8. CLEAN UP** when you're done. Put away ingredients, wipe down countertops, and wash your baking and decorating tools.

## Equivalents and Conversions

Here's a handy chart to help you convert recipe measurements.

- **1 TEASPOON** = 5 milliliters
- **1 TABLESPOON** = 3 teaspoons (or ½ fluid ounce) = 15 milliliters
- **¼ CUP** = 4 tablespoons = 60 milliliters
- **½ CUP** = 4 ounces = 120 milliliters
- **1 CUP** = 8 ounces = 240 milliliters
- **1 PINT** = 2 cups = 16 ounces = 480 milliliters
- **1 QUART** = 2 pints = 0.95 liters

## How to Store Cupcakes

Store cupcakes in a covered container. Most cupcakes can be kept at room temperature for up to 1 day and can be refrigerated for an additional 2 days. You can also store baked, undecorated cupcakes in an airtight container in the freezer for up to 1 month.

Welcome to Cupcake Class

# Have the Right Tools

To make the cupcakes in this book, you'll need the right equipment. You won't need everything shown here for every batch, but these items are all useful additions to your decorating tool kit. You can find most of them in a craft or kitchen store, or even a large grocery store.

Regular and mini muffin tins

Piping bags

Kitchen scissors

Mini food cutters

Rubber spatula

Mini offset spatula

Baking cups

Silicone candy molds

*This cupcake kit belongs to*

## DIY Decorating Kit

Make a personal cupcake decorating kit! Put your favorite baking tools in a container with a lid, then add a name label from the back of the book.

**Welcome to Cupcake Class** 13

# Stock Up on Decorations

Look through the recipes in this book and pick a few you'd like to try. Make a list of the ingredients you'll need to complete the designs. Most of the edible decorations in this book can be found wherever candy, cookies, and sprinkles are sold. If you can't find ingredients locally, ask an adult to help you purchase what you need online.

Welcome to Cupcake Class  15

# Very Vanilla Cupcakes

This classic yellow batter makes sweet, buttery cupcakes that taste better than ones from a mix. It's a good base for any decorated cupcake. Vanilla and chocolate (see page 18) cupcakes are the standard recipes, but you can experiment with flavoring them. Add some lemon or almond extract to this recipe, for example.

**Makes 12 Cupcakes (24 mini)**

- ½ cup (1 stick) butter, at room temperature
- 1 cup sugar
- 2 eggs, at room temperature
- 1½ teaspoons vanilla extract
- 1½ cups flour
- 1½ teaspoons baking powder
- Pinch of salt
- ⅔ cup buttermilk (or ⅔ cup milk + 2 teaspoons lemon juice or vinegar)

**Makes 24 Cupcakes (48 mini)**

- 1 cup (2 sticks) butter, at room temperature
- 2 cups sugar
- 4 eggs, at room temperature
- 1 tablespoon vanilla extract
- 3 cups flour
- 1 tablespoon baking powder
- ¼ teaspoon salt
- 1⅓ cups buttermilk (or 1¼ cups milk + 4 teaspoons lemon juice or vinegar)

**1.**

**Preheat the oven** to 350°F (180°C). Line a muffin tin with baking cups.

**2.**

**With a hand or stand mixer** set at a medium speed, beat the butter and sugar until light and fluffy, about 5 minutes. Add the eggs, one at a time, and beat to combine. Blend in the vanilla.

**3.**

**In a separate bowl,** whisk together the flour, baking powder, and salt. With the mixer on low, add half of the flour mixture to the butter mixture, and blend. Blend in half of the buttermilk. Add the remaining flour mixture, followed by the remaining buttermilk, beating after each addition until just combined. Scrape down the sides of the bowl as needed.

**4.**

**Using an ice cream scoop or large spoon, fill each baking cup** about two-thirds full with batter. Bake for 20 minutes (15 minutes for mini), or until a toothpick inserted in the center of a cupcake comes out clean. Remove from the pan and cool completely on a rack before decorating.

**Welcome to Cupcake Class**

# One-Bowl Chocolate Cupcakes

If you love chocolate cupcakes, here's a deliciously easy version made with cocoa powder. You can add flavor to this batter, just like the vanilla recipe on page 16. For example, a few drops of mint extract in chocolate batter produces Peppermint Patty Cupcakes—yum! What other flavors can you come up with?

### Makes 12 Cupcakes (or 24 mini)

- 1½ cups flour
- 1 cup sugar
- 6 tablespoons unsweetened cocoa powder
- 1 teaspoon baking soda
- ½ teaspoon salt
- 1 cup water
- 6 tablespoons vegetable oil
- 1 tablespoon white vinegar
- 1 teaspoon vanilla extract

### Makes 24 Cupcakes (or 48 mini)

- 3 cups flour
- 2 cups sugar
- ¾ cup unsweetened cocoa powder
- 2 teaspoons baking soda
- 1 teaspoon salt
- 2 cups water
- ¾ cup vegetable oil
- 2 tablespoons white vinegar
- 2 teaspoons vanilla extract

## BAKING SAFETY TIPS

- **Before you turn on the oven,** check first with an adult. They can show you the proper way to use it and explain its settings.
- **Arrange the oven racks** so that one is in the center. Cupcakes bake most evenly in the middle of the oven.
- **Let the oven heat** to the right temperature before you bake. Otherwise, your cupcakes will bake unevenly or take extra time to cook.
- **Always set a timer,** and don't leave the kitchen while your cupcakes are baking.
- **Always use potholders** when taking muffin tins in and out of the oven.
- **Leave the oven door shut.** The temperature drops every time the door is opened, so it should stay closed. If your oven has a light, turn it on to keep an eye on what's inside.
- **Be cautious** when you open the oven. A blast of heat will escape as soon as the door is open. Pause for a few seconds before reaching in to avoid letting it hit your face.
- **Don't forget to turn off the oven** once you're done baking.

1. **Preheat the oven** to 350°F (180°C). Line a muffin tin with baking cups.

2. **In a large bowl,** whisk together the flour, sugar, cocoa powder, baking soda, and salt.

3. **Add the water,** vegetable oil, vinegar, and vanilla, and whisk until nice and smooth.

4. **Fill each baking cup** about two-thirds full with batter. Bake for 25 minutes (15 for mini cupcakes), or until a toothpick inserted in the center of a cupcake comes out clean.

# Buttercream Frosting

This sweet, smooth frosting is perfect for cupcakes. It makes enough to decorate a dozen. Tint the whole batch a favorite color, or color portions of it to pipe on decorative swirls and designs (see page 29).

**Here's What You Need for 2 Cups**

- 1 cup (2 sticks) butter, at room temperature
- 3¾ cups confectioners' sugar
- 1 teaspoon vanilla extract
- 2–4 tablespoons milk

**1.**

**With a hand or stand mixer** set at a medium speed, beat the butter until it's light and creamy.

**2.**

**With the mixer** on low speed, add the confectioners' sugar a little at a time. Blend well.

**3.**

**Blend in the vanilla** and 2 tablespoons milk. If necessary, add more milk, 1 teaspoon at a time, to reach your desired consistency.

### SAFETY TIP

Keep your fingers out of the way of the beaters when working with an electric mixer.

**FOR CHOCOLATE FROSTING,** follow the recipe at left, but SUBSTITUTE **1 cup unsweetened cocoa powder** for 1 cup of the confectioners' sugar.

Welcome to Cupcake Class  **21**

**After you've learned a few basic techniques,** you can use the recipe photos as a starting point to create your own cupcake designs. Try substituting candies or mixing in other decorating ingredients to invent your own edible masterpieces. The sky's the limit!

**Here are a couple of tips before you start.**
- Set up a cupcake decorating station. You can use a large baking sheet or tray to hold bowls of colored frosting and other decorating ingredients. Think of them as your painter's palette!
- Practice using a piping bag and piping tip on a sheet of parchment paper before you start decorating. Follow the instructions on page 27 to learn how to pipe swirls and dots.

## Design Difficulty

Each cupcake design is rated with one, two, or three piping bags. Start with the easier projects and work your way to the more complicated ones.

### 1 PIPING BAG

These recipes are quick and easy to make with ingredients you can find at the supermarket.

### 2 PIPING BAGS

These recipes require a piping bag, piping tips, and a few basic skills.

### 3 PIPING BAGS

These recipes call for a few extra tools or special ingredients (like candy melts) and take more time to put together.

# HOW TO TINT FROSTING

Liquid      Gel

**1. Divide the frosting into bowls,** one for each color. Add a few drops of food coloring to each bowl. Use a spoon or spatula to evenly blend in the color. Scrape the bottom of the bowl as you work to make sure all the color is blended in.

**2. Gel food colors** produce more vibrant hues. Add a tiny dab or drop at first (use a toothpick if your colors are in small pots)—a little goes a long way!

## WORKING WITH STORE-BOUGHT FROSTING

Homemade frosting is hands-down delicious, but if you'd like to get right to decorating, store-bought frosting is a time-saver. Plus, it can be piped easily with a piping bag. Follow these tips for best results.

- Experiment with different store-bought brands and flavors. They each have different qualities, and you may prefer one brand over another.
- Keep in mind that different frosting flavors have different hues. Buttercreams and vanilla frosting typically have a yellowish tint. Milk chocolate-flavored frostings are usually lighter than dark chocolate varieties.
- To make colored frosting, start with white (not vanilla) frosting, so its color doesn't affect the results of your chosen tint.
- Refrigerate the frosting before using. It's easier to pipe and spread when it's chilled.

**Dark chocolate**      **Milk chocolate**      **Vanilla**      **White**

# Color Mixing Chart

You need four basic food colors and two types of frosting to make the hues listed here. Use different amounts of each to achieve different shades.

**Red + White = Pink**

**Chocolate Frosting + Vanilla Frosting = Tan**

**Black + White = Gray**

**Red + Blue = Purple**

**Yellow + Red = Orange**

**Blue + Yellow = Green**

Develop Your Decorating Skills

# HOW TO FROST A CUPCAKE

Start with a completely cooled cupcake. If you frost it while it's still warm, the frosting will melt! You can refrigerate your cupcakes before decorating to help prevent crumbling when you frost them.

For 12 cupcakes, you'll need 2 cups homemade frosting or a 16-ounce container of store-bought frosting. Having a little extra is always nice for finger licking!

**1. Use a mini offset spatula** to scoop up 1½ to 2 tablespoons of frosting, depending on the design. That's about the size of a large walnut.

**2. Start with a dollop of frosting** in the center of your cupcake, then use the end of your spatula to push and spread it out to the edges in a circular motion. If the spatula becomes too gooey, wipe it with a paper towel, or scrape away the excess frosting on the side of your frosting container.

## One at a Time

For most techniques in this book, it's best to frost and decorate one cupcake at a time. That's because the frosting begins to set after you spread it; after a few minutes, it loses the slight tackiness that helps the decorations stick to the cupcake.

**Develop Your Decorating Skills**

# WORKING WITH A PIPING BAG AND TIPS

With a piping bag, a few piping tips, and some frosting, you can create all kinds of playful designs. Follow the instructions below for assembling the bag, filling it with frosting, and adding the tips. We recommend a 12-inch disposable bag for the easiest handling.

## ASSEMBLE A PIPING BAG

**1. Snip ½ to 1 inch** (depending on the size of your tip) from the pointed end of a piping bag. Be careful not to snip off too much! Unscrew the ring from the coupler, set it aside, and slide the other half of the coupler inside the bag until its tip is through the hole.

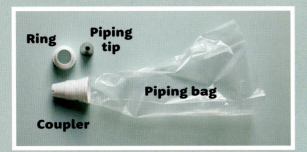

**2. Fit your chosen piping tip** on the coupler on the outside of the bag.

**3. Twist the coupler ring** over the tip to secure the tip in place.

Develop Your Decorating Skills

# FILL IT WITH FROSTING

**1.**

**Put the bag** in a tall drinking glass tip-side down and cuff the open end of the bag over the sides of the glass. Use a spoon or spatula to fill the bag with frosting.

**2.**

**Squeeze the frosting** toward the tip end of the bag, then tightly twist the open end of the bag to get rid of excess air. (You can use a twist tie or rubber band to keep the bag closed.)

# PIPE AWAY!

**1.**

**Rest the twisted end** of the bag between your thumb and forefinger and pinch them together to secure the end of the bag in your hand.

**2.**

**Use your other fingers** and palm to squeeze the frosting from the bag onto your cupcake.

**Develop Your Decorating Skills**

# DECORATING WITH PIPING TIPS

You can tell the piping tips apart by their shapes, names, and numbers. Be aware that different brands of piping tips use different numbering and labeling systems.

### WRITING TIP
Use this tiny round tip for writing messages, drawing, or outlining shapes and making small dots.

### STAR TIP
Use this tip to make a festive border, mini flowers, or a swirled design on a cupcake. Regular star tips create ribbed lines, while lines piped with a closed star are frillier.

### LARGE OR JUMBO ROUND TIP
You can make polka dot borders with this tip, draw thick lines, or create a swirl on top of a cupcake.

### GRASS TIP
This tip has several tiny, round holes on its top. Use it for making grass, animal fur, or hair.

# Candy Decoration Skills

Many of the cupcake designs in this book call for some basic prep work before you start decorating, like melting candy melts or crushing graham crackers. Here are instructions for commonly used techniques.

## USING CANDY MELTS

**1. Put the candy melts** in a microwave-safe bowl or glass measuring cup with a spout. Heat on high for 1 minute. Stir well to help the candy melt evenly.

**2. Continue to heat in 10-second bursts,** stirring vigorously after each heating, until melted.

## SAFETY TIPS

To melt candies and chocolate, you'll need to use a microwave oven. Different microwave ovens have different directions, so ask an adult to show you how to use yours.

Always use microwave-safe dishes. Glass, paper towels, and some plastic containers are fine. Never use metal or aluminum foil in the microwave. The wrong material could damage the microwave or even cause a fire.

**Develop Your Decorating Skills**

## USING A CANDY MOLD

**1. If you haven't melted** the candy wafers (or chocolate) in a cup with a spout, spoon them into a piping bag with a corner snipped off. Pipe or pour the candy or chocolate into each cup in the mold, filling it just below the fill line.

**2. Gently tap the mold** on your work surface to smooth the tops of the candy in each mold. If the mold is flexible rather than rigid, gently shake it from side to side without lifting it.

**3. Refrigerate** until the candy or chocolate is set, 10 to 15 minutes. Larger molds may take longer to set. Carefully pop out the shaped candies or chocolates from the mold.

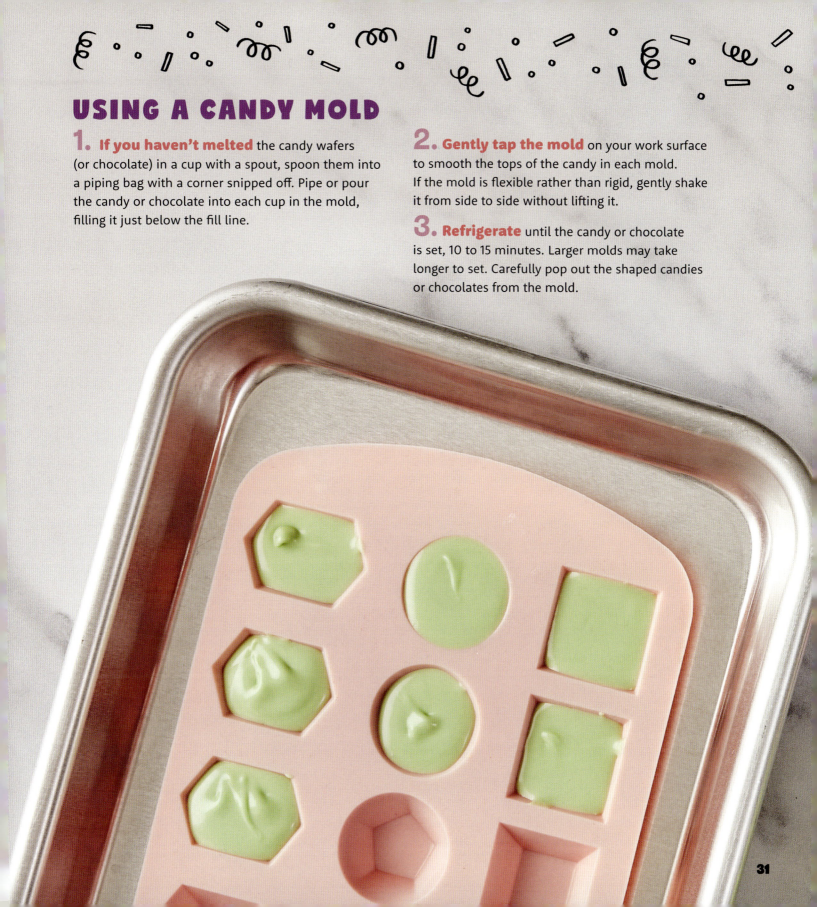

## MAKING CANDY SHAPES

To cut shapes from soft candies like gumdrops or caramels, first sprinkle a cutting board with sugar to prevent stickiness. Use confectioners' sugar for fruit chews, chocolate chews, and caramels; use granulated sugar for gumdrops and other sugar-coated candies.

**1. Knead the candy** with your fingers to flatten it. Place the flattened candy on top of the sugar and roll it with a rolling pin to make it even thinner.

**2. Cut the candy** into your desired shape with clean scissors or a paring knife. You can also use mini food cutters to make shapes.

### SAFETY TIP

Use a properly sharpened knife to cut candies (dull knives are more dangerous because they can slip while you're cutting). Hold the knife firmly with your fingers out of the way of the blade.

## CUTTING MARSHMALLOWS

Using a clean pair of kitchen scissors, cut a regular marshmallow in half crosswise to make animal snouts. To make two flower petals or a pair of insect wings, cut a mini marshmallow in half on the diagonal. You can dip the cut side of each piece in sanding sugar or sprinkles to add color.

## TRIMMING SOUR TAPE

Lay the tape flat on the cutting board. To make a tongue, cut a shape that is flat on one end and rounded on the other. Snip bits of the tape to make lines that can be used for hair, legs, or tentacles.

### Making Cookie Crumb Dirt or Graham Cracker Sand

Put cookies or crackers in a sealable plastic bag. Use a rolling pin or your hands to crush the cookies or crackers into crumbs. Alternatively, you can put the ingredients in a food processor and pulse in short bursts to get the desired consistency. To make 1 cup of crumbs, use 6 graham crackers or 12 chocolate wafers or sandwich cookies.

Develop Your Decorating Skills

# Working with Fondant

Fondant is a claylike substance made of sugar and water. You can shape it like playdough into worms, wings, doors, or anything you'd like to put on a cupcake or work into your designs. If you can't find a special shaped candy, make it yourself out of fondant! You can buy fondant at any store that sells cake decorating supplies. Here are a few tips for using fondant.

- For best results, buy small packages of fondant in the colors you'd like to use. You can color white fondant on your own with food coloring, but it's easier and less messy to just buy the fondant already colored. You can find it in just about any color, even shimmery ones.

- Remove a small portion of the fondant from the package. (Keep the remaining fondant covered and sealed so that it doesn't dry out.) Knead it with your hands to soften it.

- Try rolling it into balls like the planets on page 84.

- For a marble effect, knead two or more colors of fondant together to form a swirling pattern, then shape as desired.

- To make flat shapes, roll the fondant out with a rolling pin, then use cookie or fondant cutters or a paring knife to cut out shapes.

- To attach pieces together, brush each with a small bit of water and press them in place. Let dry for at least 15 minutes.

# MAKING A FONDANT TWISTY ROPE

Twisting a rope of fondant together produces a fun effect. Use two colors to make a unicorn horn (page 104). What else can you think of to make?

ta-da!

**1. Knead a portion** of fondant until it's soft. Roll it into a thin rope.

**2. Fold the rope to form a U.** Starting at the middle, wind the sides together to make a twisted length.

**3. Secure the ends** by pinching them together.

Develop Your Decorating Skills

# 3

# Sprinkles, Dots & Squiggles

**Calling all cupcake artists!** You need only a few simple ingredients to turn a plain cupcake into a sweet masterpiece. With sprinkles and a piping bag filled with frosting you can doodle and decorate to your heart's delight.

# ALL ABOUT SPRINKLES

One of the simplest ways to decorate cupcakes is to cover them with sprinkles. You can buy sprinkles wherever baking supplies are sold, in all sorts of colors, shapes, and sizes.

## SANDING SUGAR
Fine sugar crystals available in a variety of colors

## COARSE SUGAR
Larger sugar crystals

## SUGAR PEARLS
Colored balls with a pearly finish, typically available in light colors

## NONPAREILS
Teensy balls in a variety of colors and color mixes

## SPRINKLES OR JIMMIES
Tube-shaped pieces available in thick and thin varieties

## SPECIAL SHAPES
Sprinkles in shapes such as mini stars, jumbo hearts, birds, flowers, and holiday shapes like Halloween ghosts and pumpkins, winter snowflakes, Christmas trees, or Easter bunnies

## NONTRADITIONAL
Small candies like mini mints, bubblegum, chocolate gems, and mini candy rocks

## CONFETTI
Flat, round coins available in sizes from very small to jumbo

Sprinkles, Dots & Squiggles

### GET CREATIVE!

Frost a cupcake and sprinkle it with nonpareils, mini rainbow shapes, confetti, or any edible sweet. You can even dip a cupcake into orange sanding sugar and top with a peppermint leaf gumdrop to make an orange.

Sprinkles, Dots & Squiggles  39

# Sugar Stenciled

Use the stencils from the back of the book to create fun patterns and shapes on your cupcakes with sprinkles or colored sugar. Small sprinkles like nonpareils and sanding sugar work best.

### Here's What You Need

- 12 cupcakes
- 2 cups white frosting
- Stencils (page 145)
- Nonpareil sprinkles or sanding sugar

**1. Top a cupcake** with an even layer of frosting, about 2 tablespoons. (It's best to frost and decorate one cupcake at a time.) Put the cupcake on a sheet of parchment paper. Choose a stencil and gently rest it on the frosting.

**2. Scatter sprinkles** over the stencil to fill in the design. Carefully remove the stencil to reveal the pattern.

**3. Move the decorated cupcake** to a serving dish. Keep your work area clean by folding the parchment paper and pouring the leftover sprinkles back into the container. Frost and decorate the remaining cupcakes.

Sprinkles, Dots & Squiggles

# Hip, Hip, Hooray!

Here's a cheery way to celebrate a birthday or other special event: Say "Hip, hip, hooray" using store-bought cookies, frosting, and colorful sprinkles.

**Here's What You Need**

- 12 cupcakes
- 2 cups white frosting
- Piping bag fitted with a writing tip
- Yellow food coloring
- Alphabet cookies
- Sprinkles

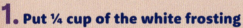

**1. Put ¼ cup of the white frosting** in the piping bag. In a medium bowl, tint the remaining frosting yellow. Top a cupcake with an even layer of yellow frosting, about 2 tablespoons. (It's best to frost and decorate one cupcake at a time.)

**2. Pick out cookie letters** to spell Hip Hip Hooray or a special person's name (there should be 12 letters or fewer). Pipe white frosting onto each letter.

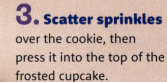

**3. Scatter sprinkles** over the cookie, then press it into the top of the frosted cupcake.

**4. Frost and decorate** the remaining cookies and cupcakes. Arrange the cupcakes to spell your message and let the party begin!

Sprinkles, Dots & Squiggles 43

# Squiggles & Dots

The decorations on these freestyle sweets are made using a small writing tip. Even better, the technique is a piece of cake!

**Here's What You Need**

- 12 cupcakes
- 2½ cups white frosting
- Food coloring in four different hues
- 4 piping bags fitted with writing tips

**1. Divide the frosting** into four small bowls (a heaping ½ cup in each). Tint each bowl with one of the colors of food coloring.

**2. Top the cupcakes** with a thin, even layer of frosting, about 1 heaping tablespoon of frosting per cupcake. Frost three cupcakes with each color. Put the remaining frosting into the piping bags.

Sprinkles, Dots & Squiggles

**3. To make dots,** hold the piping bag vertically atop a cupcake and squeeze the frosting out of the bag without moving the tip until a small circle is formed.

**4. Pipe squiggles,** lines, and dots on each cupcake with a contrasting color of frosting.

Sprinkles, Dots & Squiggles   45

# Number 8 Cake

How old are you now? Say it with a batch of birthday cupcakes in a clever arrangement. Depending on the number you want to make, you might need two dozen cupcakes.

**Here's What You Need**

- 12–24 cupcakes
- 2 cups white frosting
- Food coloring in four different hues
- 4 piping bags fitted with round or star tips in various sizes

**1. Divide the frosting** into four bowls (½ cup in each). Tint each bowl with one of the colors of food coloring. Put each color of frosting in a separate piping bag.

**2. Pipe dollops or stars** of frosting on each cupcake. To make the dollops, hold a piping bag fitted with a round tip vertically atop a cupcake and squeeze the frosting out of the bag without moving the tip until a small dollop is formed. Use the same technique with a star tip to make stars.

**3. You can also use a star tip** to make swirls. Holding the piping bag vertically, pipe a circle of frosting your desired size, then continue piping in a circular motion, without lifting the tip, until the shape is filled.

Sprinkles, Dots & Squiggles

**4. Arrange the cupcakes** on a platter in the shape of the number representing your age.

Sprinkles, Dots & Squiggles 47

# Rainbows & Marshmallow Clouds

Add some color to a cloudy day! With this special frosting-spreading technique, you can turn an ordinary cupcake into a rainbow-colored work of art.

### Here's What You Need

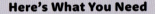

- 12 cupcakes
- 2 cups white frosting
- Blue, red, yellow, and green food coloring
- 4 piping bags fitted with writing tips
- 36 mini marshmallows, cut in half crosswise

**1.** **Put 1 cup of the frosting** in a small bowl and tint it blue. Evenly divide the remaining frosting among four bowls (¼ cup each) and tint the frosting red, yellow, orange, and green (see the color mixing chart on page 25). Put the red, yellow, orange, and green frosting in the piping bags.

**2.** **Top a cupcake** with a thin layer of blue frosting, about 1 tablespoon. (It's best to frost and decorate one cupcake at a time.) Pipe a line of red frosting around half of the outer edge of the cupcake. Add a line of orange directly below the red, followed by one yellow and one green line.

**48**  Sprinkles, Dots & Squiggles

**3.** **Starting at one end** of the rainbow, use a mini offset spatula to carefully sweep over the lines and blend them together.

**4.** **Place six marshmallow halves** for clouds below the rainbow. Frost and decorate the remaining cupcakes.

Sprinkles, Dots & Squiggles     **49**

# 4
# Animals, Animals Everywhere!

**From sleepy sloths to roaring lions,** these cupcake designs are great for all animal lovers. Create a pack of "pup cakes," a school of gummy fish, a bunch of adorable pandas, and many more!

50

# Goodie Golden Retriever

The furry-textured frosting on these canine cakes is made with a grass piping tip. With a pack of these to share, you're sure to make at least a few loyal friends.

### Here's What You Need
- 12 cupcakes
- 1½ cups white frosting
- ½ cup chocolate frosting
- Yellow food coloring
- Piping bag fitted with a grass tip
- 6 regular marshmallows
- 2 or 3 strips red sour tape
- 12 soft caramel candies
- 24 brown chocolate gems
- 12 black jellybeans

**1. Add the white frosting** and the chocolate frosting to a medium bowl and tint it with a few drops of the food coloring to make a tan color. Put the frosting in the piping bag.

**2. Cut each marshmallow** in half crosswise. Cut the sour tape into 12 pieces and trim each piece into the shape of a tongue. Knead and flatten the caramels with your fingers. Trim each one into two ears.

**3. Use a dot of frosting** to attach a marshmallow half to a cupcake. (It's best to frost and decorate one cupcake at a time.)

**4. Pipe frosting onto the cupcake,** covering the whole surface and the marshmallow.

52  Animals, Animals Everywhere!

**5.** **Add a pair of chocolate gem eyes** and a jellybean nose. Press the ears in place. Finish the face with a sour tape tongue. Frost and decorate the remaining cupcakes.

# A PACK OF PUP CAKES!

Your friends won't be able to keep their paws off these cute pooches.

## Golden Retriever

Chocolate Frosting Fur +
Halved Marshmallow Muzzle +
Black Jellybean Nose +
Soft Caramel Ears +
Chocolate Gem Eyes +
Sour Tape Tongue (see page 52)

## Poodle

White Frosting Fur +
White Frosting Ears and Hair Piped with Star Tip +
Halved Marshmallow Muzzle +
Black Jellybean Nose +
Chocolate Gem Eyes +
Bow Sprinkles

## Paw Print

Mini Cupcake +
White Frosting +
Mini Round Chocolate Peppermint Paw +
Chocolate Gem Pads

54    Animals, Animals Everywhere!

## Dalmatian
White Frosting with
  Chocolate Frosting Spots +
Halved Marshmallow Muzzle +
Black Jellybean Nose +
Chocolate Almond and
  White Jordan Almond Ears +
Sour Tape Tongue +
Chocolate Gem Eyes

## Chocolate Lab
Chocolate Frosting Fur +
Halved Marshmallow Muzzle +
Black Jellybean Nose +
Chocolate Almond Ears +
Chocolate Gem Eyes +
Sour Tape Tongue

## Jack Russell Terrier
White Frosting Fur +
Halved Marshmallow Muzzle +
Black Jellybean Nose +
Almond Ears +
Sour Tape Tongue +
Chocolate Gem Eyes

Animals, Animals Everywhere!

# Calico Kitty

A wooden toothpick or small bamboo skewer is the *purr-fect* tool for creating a furry effect on these felines. You can also use the tines of a fork.

### Here's What You Need

- 12 cupcakes
- 1 cup white frosting
- 1 cup chocolate frosting
- 12 white gumdrops
- 24 brown mini chocolate gems
- 24 brown chocolate gems
- Mini heart sprinkles
- White sprinkles

**1. In a medium bowl,** stir together ⅓ cup each of the white and chocolate frosting. Place the remaining white and chocolate frosting in separate small bowls. Cut each gumdrop in half lengthwise.

**2. Top a cupcake** with about 2 teaspoons of each color frosting. (It's best to frost and decorate one cupcake at a time.)

**3. Use the tip of a toothpick** or bamboo skewer to spread and lift the frosting, so that it forms little peaks of fur.

**56**  Animals, Animals Everywhere!

**4. Add a pair of mini chocolate** gem eyes and a pair of regular chocolate gems for the muzzle. Add a mini heart sprinkle nose. (You can use tweezers to place them perfectly.)

**5. Finish the kitten's face** with white sprinkle whiskers. Press on two gumdrop ears. Frost and decorate the remaining cupcakes.

Animals, Animals Everywhere! 57

# Candy Panda

You won't find real pandas living in a group, but this inspired version is a delight with a dozen of them arranged together.

### Here's What You Need

- 12 cupcakes
- 24 black or purple gumdrops
- Granulated sugar
- 2 cups white frosting
- 24 mini brown chocolate gems
- 12 mini black jellybeans
- ⅓ cup coarse sugar or shredded coconut

**1. Cut 12 of the gumdrops** in half lengthwise for ears. Sprinkle a cutting board with granulated sugar. Use a rolling pin to flatten the remaining gumdrops to about ⅛ inch thick. Use a mini oval cutter or kitchen scissors to cut each into two or more ovals (you'll need a total of 24).

**2. Top a cupcake** with an even layer of frosting, about 2 tablespoons. (It's best to frost and decorate one cupcake at a time.)

**3. Position a pair** of gumdrop ovals to make the eye masks. Top each with a dot of frosting. Lightly press a chocolate gem onto the frosting so that the frosting shows around the edges.

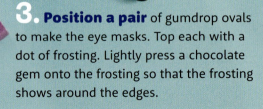

**4. Add a black jellybean** nose and two gumdrop ears. Sprinkle with coarse sugar. Frost and decorate the remaining cupcakes.

# Choc-o-Sloth

Use chocolate frosting for the fur of these tree-hugging treats. For even more scrumptiousness, make them with a chocolate cupcake base.

**Here's What You Need**

- 12 cupcakes
- 3 chocolate chews
- 2 cups chocolate frosting
- Piping bag fitted with a grass tip
- 12 vanilla wafers
- 24 black pearl sprinkles
- 12 mini chocolate gems

**1. Use a rolling pin to flatten the chocolate chews,** then cut out four ovals for the eye masks. Pinch one end of each oval into a point, as shown. Reserve ¼ cup of the frosting in a small bowl and put the remaining frosting in the piping bag. Dot the center of a cupcake with frosting and attach a vanilla wafer for the sloth's face. (It's best to frost and decorate one cupcake at a time.)

Animals, Animals Everywhere!

**2. With a toothpick,** add a few dabs of frosting to the center of the cookie and top with two eye mask pieces.

**3. Add a dot of frosting** on each eye mask, then attach two pearl sprinkle eyes. Add another dot of frosting below the eye mask and attach a mini chocolate gem nose.

**4. Pipe on the sloth's hair,** working your way around the edge of the cookie. Dot a tuft at the top of the head. Use a toothpick to add a line of frosting for a mouth. Frost and decorate the remaining cupcakes.

**Animals, Animals Everywhere!**

# Roaring Lion

The majestic manes and friendly faces on these cats will keep any crowd roaring for more.

### Here's What You Need

- 12 cupcakes
- 2 cups white frosting
- Red and yellow food coloring
- ¼ cup chocolate frosting
- Piping bag fitted with a writing tip
- 12 vanilla wafers
- 24 butterscotch or peanut butter chips
- Orange sprinkles
- 12 brown or black jellybeans

**1. In a medium bowl,** tint the white frosting with the food coloring (mixing red and yellow to make orange). Put the chocolate frosting in the piping bag.

**2. Top a cupcake** with an even layer of orange frosting, about 2 tablespoons. (It's best to frost and decorate one cupcake at a time.)

**3. Add a vanilla wafer** to the center. Press a pair of butterscotch chip ears into place.

**4.** **Working on top of a sheet** of parchment paper to catch spills, scatter orange sprinkles on the frosting around the edge of the cookie.

**5.** **With the chocolate frosting,** pipe on a pair of eyes. Add another small dot of frosting to attach a jellybean nose and draw a line of frosting for the muzzle. Frost and decorate the remaining cupcakes.

Animals, Animals Everywhere!

# Frog on a Log

These aren't the same little speckled frogs that sat on a speckled log, but you can bet they'll disappear one by one, just like the ones in the nursery song!

**Here's What You Need**

- 12 cupcakes
- 1½ cups white frosting
- Green food coloring
- ¼ cup chocolate frosting
- Piping bag fitted with a writing tip
- 12 pretzel sticks
- 24 peppermint leaf gumdrops
- 24 mini green jellybeans
- 24 jumbo candy eyes

**1. In a medium bowl,** tint the white frosting with the food coloring. Put the chocolate frosting in the piping bag.

**2. Top a cupcake** with an even layer of green frosting, about 2 tablespoons. (It's best to frost and decorate one cupcake at a time.)

**3. Arrange a pretzel stick** at the bottom of the cupcake. Add a pair of peppermint leaf legs, jellybean feet, and a pair of candy eyes.

Animals, Animals Everywhere!

**4.** **Use the chocolate frosting** to pipe on a mouth and nostrils. Frost and decorate the remaining cupcakes.

Animals, Animals Everywhere!  65

# Gumdrop Dinosaur

Future paleontologists will love discovering these prehistoric dinosaurs at a birthday party. They're made with purple and green gumdrops, but you can choose any color candies you'd like!

**Here's What You Need**

- 12 cupcakes
- 2 cups white frosting
- ½ cup chocolate frosting
- Piping bag fitted with a writing tip
- 60 small gumdrops
- 24 mini jellybeans
- 12 candy fruit slices

**1. In a medium bowl,** tint the white frosting with ¼ cup chocolate frosting to make it light brown. Put the remaining chocolate frosting in the piping bag. Trim away the bottom of each gumdrop for the dino's spikes and head, and cut each jellybean in half crosswise for the feet.

**2. Top a cupcake** with an even layer of light brown frosting, about 2 tablespoons. (It's best to frost and decorate one cupcake at a time.)

**3. Press on a fruit slice body.** Add a gumdrop head and three gumdrop spikes cut-side down.

Animals, Animals Everywhere!

**4. Use the chocolate frosting** to pipe on two eyes and nostrils.

**5. Arrange four jellybean feet** on the sides of the dinosaur body. Frost and decorate the remaining cupcakes.

Animals, Animals Everywhere! **67**

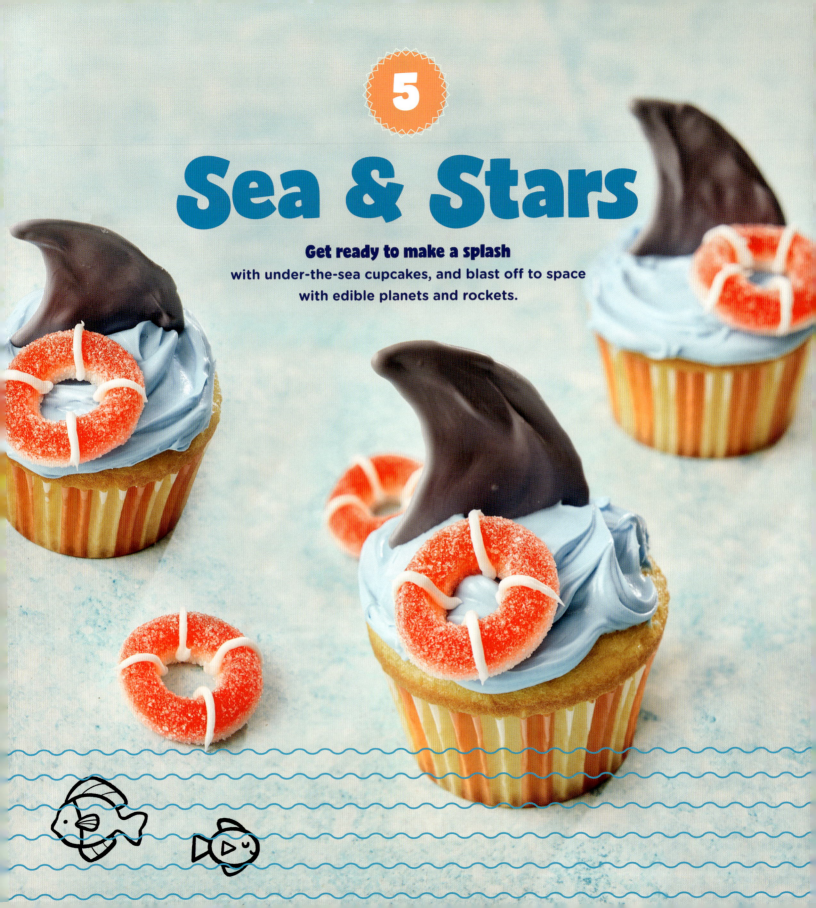

# 5

# Sea & Stars

**Get ready to make a splash** with under-the-sea cupcakes, and blast off to space with edible planets and rockets.

# Sail Away!

Make waves at an under-the-sea party with a seafaring sweet! You'll spot the sails for each mini vessel in the back of this book.

**Here's What You Need**
- 12 cupcakes
- 2 cups white frosting
- Blue food coloring
- 12 sticker sails from the back of the book
- 12 toothpicks
- 12 candy fruit slices
- 12 gummy bears or teddy grahams

**1. In a medium bowl,** tint the frosting with the food coloring. Fold each sticker sail around a toothpick and insert one in each candy fruit slice.

**2. Top a cupcake** with an even layer of frosting, about 2 tablespoons. (It's best to frost and decorate one cupcake at a time.) Press a candy fruit slice boat onto the frosted cupcake.

**3.** **Attach a gummy bear** to the boat with a dot of frosting. Frost and decorate the remaining cupcakes.

# School of Cool

Use this clever technique for creating a group of rainbow fish or skip ahead to step 4 and top your frosted cupcakes with plain candy fish. Either way, they're sure to be a swimming success!

### Here's What You Need

- 24 mini cupcakes
- 24–48 gummy fish candies in multiple colors
- ½ cup white chocolate chips
- Confetti sprinkles for eyes
- 2 cups white frosting
- Blue food coloring
- White nonpareil sprinkles (optional)

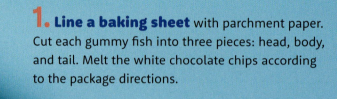

**1. Line a baking sheet** with parchment paper. Cut each gummy fish into three pieces: head, body, and tail. Melt the white chocolate chips according to the package directions.

**2. Dip the cut end** of a fish head in melted chocolate and put it on the prepared baking sheet. Press on a body piece. Dip the cut end of a fish tail in the chocolate and connect it to the body piece. (If you like, you can mix colors for the heads, bodies, and tails.) Repeat with the remaining fish candies and melted chocolate. Add a dab of chocolate and a confetti eye to each head. Let the chocolate set.

**3. In a medium bowl,** tint the frosting with the food coloring. Top a cupcake with an even layer of frosting, about 1 tablespoon. (It's best to frost and decorate one cupcake at a time.)

72  Sea & Stars

**4.** **Add a fish** to the top of the frosted cupcake. Scatter on a pinch of nonpareil bubbles, if using.

**5.** **Frost and decorate** the remaining cupcakes.

# Rainbow Jellyfish

The long tentacles on these jellyfish cupcakes are made from snips of tangy rainbow sour tape—all sugar and no sting!

### Here's What You Need

- 12 cupcakes
- 2 cups white frosting
- Blue food coloring
- 4 strips rainbow sour tape
- 12 mini fruit slice candies
- 24 candy eyes
- White nonpareil sprinkles
- Mini fish-shaped sprinkles

**1. In a medium bowl,** tint the frosting with the food coloring. Cut the sour tape crosswise into 48 thin strips.

**2. Top a cupcake** with an even layer of frosting, about 2 tablespoons. (It's best to frost and decorate one cupcake at a time.) Add a fruit slice head and four sour tape tentacles.

**3.** **Use a toothpick** to add small dots of frosting to the head, then attach candy eyes.

**4. Scatter on nonpareil bubbles** and fish sprinkles. Frost and decorate the remaining cupcakes.

Sea & Stars   **75**

# Shark Fins

Something scary is circling on this cupcake—or so it appears. Luckily there's a fruit-ring raft to save you from whatever danger might await.

**Here's What You Need**

- 12 cupcakes
- ½ cup white candy melts
- ½ cup black candy melts
- Piping bag fitted with a large writing tip
- Shark fin template (page 143)
- 2 cups white frosting
- Blue food coloring
- Piping bag fitted with a small writing tip
- 12 gummy rings

**1. Combine the candy melts** in a microwave-safe bowl and heat on high power for 1 minute. Stir vigorously. Continue to microwave in 10-second bursts, stirring thoroughly after each, until the candy is melted. Put the melted candy in the piping bag with the large writing tip.

**2. Place a sheet of parchment paper** over the fin template. Using the template as a guide, pipe a candy shark fin onto the parchment, starting with the edges first, then filling in the center. Smooth the candy with a mini offset spatula. Repeat with the remaining candy to make 12 fins. Let the candy set at room temperature, then gently peel them off the paper.

**3. In a medium bowl,** tint 1¾ cups of the frosting with the food coloring. Put the remaining white frosting in the piping bag with the small writing tip.

**4. With the white frosting,** pipe lines onto each gummy ring.

**5. Top a cupcake** with dollop of the blue frosting, about 2 tablespoons, then use your spatula to spread the frosting into swoops across the surface. (It's best to frost and decorate one cupcake at a time.)

76  Sea & Stars

**6.** **Press a candy fin** and gummy ring inner tube in place. Frost and decorate the remaining cupcakes.

Sea & Stars 77

# Dreamy Mermaid Tails

For an undersea adventure right in your kitchen, make these magical mermaid tails out of candy melts. You'll need a candy mold, which is available at craft stores and online.

**Here's What You Need**

- 12 cupcakes
- 1 cup pink candy melts
- 1 cup purple candy melts
- Mermaid tail silicone mold
- 2 cups white frosting
- Blue food coloring
- Seashell and starfish sprinkles
- Confetti sprinkles
- Nonpareils

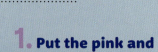

**1. Put the pink and purple candy melts** in separate microwave-safe bowls. To melt, heat each on high power for 1 minute. Stir vigorously. Continue to microwave in 10-second bursts, stirring thoroughly after each, until the candy is melted.

**2. Put the candy mold** on a baking sheet, then spoon a bit of each candy color into the wells of the silicone mold, filling each about half to three-quarters full. Use a skewer or toothpick to gently swirl the candy in each well. Gently tap the baking sheet (with the mold still on top) on your work surface to flatten the surface of the candy in each well.

**3. Refrigerate until the candy is set,** about 25 minutes, then remove the tails from the mold.

**4. In a medium bowl,** tint the frosting with the food coloring. Top a cupcake with an even layer of frosting, about 2 tablespoons, then use a mini offset spatula to make swoops over the surface. (It's best to frost and decorate one cupcake at a time.)

**5. Place a tail in the center** of the cupcake. Scatter on seashell, starfish, and confetti sprinkles, along with some nonpareils. Frost and decorate the remaining cupcakes.

SPLASH!

Sea & Stars

# Cookie Sandcastles

Treat yourself to a summer day with these small but grand towers that you can build and eat!

**Here's What You Need**

- 6 regular size cupcakes
- 12–18 mini cupcakes
- 6 graham crackers, crushed into crumbs
- 2 cups white frosting
- Cone-shaped corn snacks
- Toothpicks
- Flag stickers from the back of the book
- Seashell sprinkles
- White pearl sprinkles

**1. Put the graham cracker crumbs** in a shallow bowl. Frost a cupcake with an even layer of frosting and dip it in the crumbs to coat. Repeat with the remaining cupcakes.

80   Sea & Stars

**2. Now build some sandcastles!** Stack two mini cupcakes on top of each other, or place one mini on top of a regular cupcake. Add a corn snack and a toothpick flag for each sandcastle top.

**3. Decorate with seashell** and white pearl sprinkles to make your castles look magical!

Sea & Stars  81

# Pirate Map of Treasures

Ahoy, matey! We know the way to a spectacular pirate party. It all starts with a map made of confections (and a little extra embellishment with some surprises from the back of the book).

### Here's What You Need

- 12 cupcakes
- 6 graham crackers, crushed into crumbs
- 2 cups white frosting
- 1 strip red sour tape
- Black licorice lace
- Skulls and bones sprinkles
- Candy rocks
- Chocolate coins
- 1 mini chocolate nugget candy
- Gold confetti sprinkles
- Pirate flag stickers and palm tree cutouts from the back of the book

**1. Put the graham cracker crumbs** in a shallow bowl. Top each cupcake with an even layer of frosting, about 2 tablespoons, then dip it in the crumbs to coat. (See photo on page 80.)

82  Sea & Stars

**2. Arrange the cupcakes** on a platter to make a trail. Cut a dot and two strips to form an X from the sour tape. Place the dot on the cupcake at the beginning of the trail. Put the X on the cupcake at the end.

**3. Snip the licorice lace** into 1-inch pieces. Arrange the pieces in a dotted path along the cupcakes from the sour tape dot to the X. Add skulls and bones sprinkles, candy rocks, and chocolate coins along the path.

**4. Use a toothpick** to apply a bit of frosting to the flat side of the chocolate nugget. Attach gold confetti sprinkles, then add the edible treasure chest to the cupcake next to the X.

**5. Finish the map** by pressing the pirate flag stickers and palm tree cutouts in place.

Sea & Stars  83

# Planet Earth

Celebrate Earth Day any day of the year with cupcakes that look like our world. Mix blue and green fondant together for the land and water. Once you get the hang of rolling fondant, you can make other planets in the solar system (see page 86).

### Here's What You Need

- 12 cupcakes
- 1 cup (about 8 ounces) blue fondant
- ½ cup (about 4 ounces) green fondant
- 2 cups white frosting
- Blue food coloring
- Silver sanding sugar
- White nonpareils
- Star sprinkles

**1. Knead the blue and green fondants** together to represent the water and land. Roll about 1½ tablespoons of fondant into a ball to make each planet Earth.

**2. In a medium bowl,** tint the frosting with the food coloring. Top a cupcake with an even layer of frosting, about 2 tablespoons. (It's best to frost and decorate one cupcake at time.)

84  Sea & Stars

**3. Place a planet** on the cupcake. Sprinkle on sanding sugar, nonpareils, and star sprinkles. Frost and decorate the remaining cupcakes.

# AWESOME PLANETS

Expand your galaxy with more stars, moons, and planets all made with fondant. Start with a blue frosting base for each cupcake and finish your design with silver star sprinkles, sanding sugar, and white nonpareils.

### Saturn
Gold and Yellow Fondant Ball +
Gold Saturn Ring

### Neptune
Blue and Purple
Fondant Ball

### Starry Sky
Star Sprinkles +
Silver Sanding Sugar +
White Nonpareils

86  Sea & Stars

# Hard Candy Geodes

For a fun kitchen science experiment, make colorful, sparkling geodes by melting hard candies. Top cupcakes with them and tell friends to enjoy crunching up the "rocks"! (Don't bite too hard, though, or you might hurt your teeth.)

**Here's What You Need**

- 12 cupcakes
- 48 hard candies in varying colors
- Silicone cupcake mold
- Gold sparkling sugar
- Pastry brush
- 2 cups white frosting
- Black food coloring
- Candy rocks

**1.**

**Preheat the oven** to 275°F (135°C). Working with one color of hard candy at a time, gently crush each candy in its wrapper with the bottom of a glass. Unwrap the crushed candies and put each color in a separate small bowl.

**2.**

**Put a silicone cupcake mold** on a baking sheet. Spoon a little of one candy color around the edges of each well, filling it ¼ inch high. Sprinkle a contrasting candy color in the centers.

**3.**

**Bake until the candy** is completely melted, about 12 minutes. Remove the baking sheet from the oven, let the candy cool and harden for 10 minutes, then remove the geodes from the molds.

**4.**

**Line a baking sheet** with parchment paper. Put the sparkling sugar in a small bowl. Use a pastry brush to paint the edges of a geode with water, dip it in the sugar to coat the edges, then put it on the prepared baking sheet. Repeat with the remaining geodes and sugar. Let dry for 5 minutes.

Sea & Stars

**5. In a medium bowl,** tint the frosting with the food coloring to make gray. Top a cupcake with an even layer of frosting, about 2 tablespoons. (It's best to frost and decorate one cupcake at a time.)

**6. Add a geode,** shiny-side up, and press on a few candy rocks. Frost and decorate the remaining cupcakes.

# Mini Cone Rockets

Master the art of an out-of-this-world spaceship and your cupcake career may take off. If you can't find the mini cones at your grocery store, look online.

**Here's What You Need**

- 12 cupcakes
- 36 red gumdrops
- 2 cups white frosting
- Blue, red, and yellow food coloring
- 4 piping bags fitted with large round tips
- 12 mini ice cream cones
- 12 mini tart candies

**1. Cut 24 of the gumdrops** in half on the diagonal and set aside for the rocket wings. Divide the frosting into four bowls (½ cup in each). Tint each bowl a different color with the food coloring: blue, red, yellow, and orange (using a bit of each of red and yellow). Put each of the frosting colors into a separate piping bag.

**2. It's best to frost and decorate** one rocket at a time. Pipe a dot of blue frosting on the flat end of a cone. Press on a whole gumdrop. Pipe two more dots of blue frosting on the sides of the cone and attach a halved gumdrop wing to each. Use another dot of frosting to add a tart candy window.

**3. Pipe a few dollops** of red, yellow, and orange frosting around the edges of a cupcake, leaving a ¼-inch border as shown.

Sea & Stars

**4.** **Press a rocket on top** of the frosting "flames." Frost and decorate the remaining cupcakes.

# 6
# Nature Magic

**From bugs to flowers to fairies,**
bring the wonder of the natural world into your kitchen
with these outdoor-inspired cupcakes.

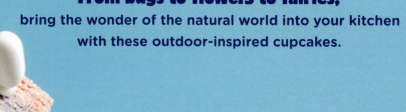

# Daisy Cakes

Brighten someone's day with a garden of daisy cupcakes! The flower petals are made from snips of sweet marshmallows.

**Here's What You Need**

- 24 mini cupcakes
- 2 cups white frosting
- Green food coloring
- Piping bag fitted with a grass tip
- 60 mini marshmallows
- 24 yellow chocolate or fruit gems

**1. In a medium bowl,** tint the frosting with the food coloring. Put the frosting in the piping bag. Use kitchen scissors to cut each of the marshmallows in half on the diagonal.

**2. Pipe green grass** on a cupcake. (It's best to frost and decorate one cupcake at a time.) Press a yellow candy gem in the center and arrange five mini marshmallows, cut-side up, around the candy. Frost and decorate the remaining cupcakes.

94   Nature Magic

# FLOWER GARDEN

Welcome spring, thank Mom on Mother's Day, or brighten up an Easter table with a colorful bouquet of pretty blooms. Start with green frosting, either spread on smoothly or piped to look like grass.

### Sunflower
Mini Chocolate Sandwich Cookie Center **+**
Halved Gumdrop Petals

### Daisy
Mini Marshmallow Petals **+**
Candy Gem Center (page 94)

### Lily
Orange Oblong Fruit Chew **+**
Yellow Gumdrop Center

96   Nature Magic

## Pansy
**Candy Gem Center +
Jordan Almond Petals**

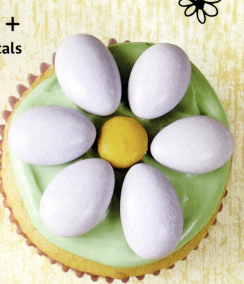

## Baby Bouquet
**Mini Candy Gem Petals and Center +
Green Sour Tape Stems and Leaves**

Nature Magic

# Ant Attack

Whether you're hosting a bug-themed party or a backyard picnic, make a batch of these brown bugs to crawl across your picnic table.

**Here's What You Need**

- 12 cupcakes
- 2 cups white frosting
- Black food coloring
- ½ cup chocolate frosting
- Piping bag fitted with a writing tip
- 24 brown chocolate gems
- 12 brown chocolate-covered peanuts or almonds

**1. In a medium bowl,** tint the white frosting with the food coloring, making gray. Put the chocolate frosting in the piping bag. Top a cupcake with an even layer of gray frosting, about 2 tablespoons. (It's best to frost and decorate one cupcake at a time.)

**2. Pipe a U shape** of chocolate frosting on top of the cupcake to mark the ant head (the tip of the U will be the antenae). Press two chocolate gem candies and a chocolate-covered nut to form the head and body.

98    Nature Magic

**3.** **Use more chocolate frosting** to pipe on legs. Frost and decorate the remaining cupcakes.

# CREEPY CRAWLERS

Make a whole menagerie of beetles, worms, and other critters. Start with some gray or brown frosting for the base. If you'd like, add cookie crumb dirt for your bugs to crawl on (see page 33).

## Centipede
Green Chocolate Gem Body +
Piped Chocolate Frosting Legs

## Ladybug
Red Chocolate Gem or
Candy Melt Body +
Black Edible Marker Spots +
Black Mini Jellybean Head +
Piped Chocolate Frosting Legs

## Dragonfly
Rolled and Trimmed
White Gumdrop Wings +
Green Oblong Fruit
Chew Body +
Green Chocolate Gem Head

Nature Magic

## Spider
Mini Chocolate Sandwich Cookie Body +
Piped Chocolate Frosting Legs +
Mini Chocolate Gem Head

## Beetle
Black Mini Jellybean Head +
Green Jordan Almond Body +
Rolled and Trimmed Green Gumdrop Wings

## Ant
Chocolate Gem Head and Body +
Chocolate-Covered Nut Abdomen +
Piped Chocolate Frosting Legs (page 98)

## Wiggly Worm
Chocolate Cookie Dirt +
Gummy Worm

Nature Magic **101**

# Slithering Snakes

Arrange these bright green frosted cupcakes into a den of edible snakes that slither across your party table. Add hissing tongues and pointed tails made of flattened gumdrops.

**Here's What You Need**

- 24 mini cupcakes
- 2 cups white frosting
- Green food coloring
- Sugar
- 2 red gumdrops
- 4 green gumdrops
- 8 mini chocolate gems
- Green, gold, and black sprinkle mix

**1. In a medium bowl,** tint the frosting with the food coloring.

**2. Sprinkle a cutting board with sugar.** Use a rolling pin to flatten each red gumdrop, then trim each into two tongues. Flatten and roll out each green gumdrop. Cut each one into triangles for the face and tail.

**3. For each snake,** arrange six of the cupcakes on a platter. (It's best to arrange, frost, and decorate one snake at a time.) Top each cupcake with an even layer of frosting, about 1 tablespoon. Add two chocolate gem eyes and a gumdrop triangle face to the head cupcake, and a gumdrop triangle tail to the tail cupcake. Scatter sprinkles across all the cupcakes.

**4. Arrange, frost, and decorate** the remaining cupcake snakes.

Nature Magic

# Mystical Unicorns

These enchanting cupcakes have edible horns made of gold and silver fondant that capture the magic of these fairy-tale creatures. You need a bit more frosting for each cupcake to achieve the swirly top.

### Here's What You Need

- 12 cupcakes
- 2¼ cups white frosting
- Red and blue food coloring
- Piping bag fitted with a star tip
- ¼ cup pink sanding sugar
- 12 mini marshmallows
- 1 (4-ounce) package silver fondant
- 1 (4-ounce) package gold fondant
- Purple and gold sprinkle mix

**1. In a medium bowl,** tint the white frosting with red and blue food coloring, making purple. Put the frosting in the piping bag.

**2. Put the sanding sugar** in a small bowl. Cut each marshmallow in half on the diagonal, then dip each half, sticky-side down, in the sanding sugar.

**3. Knead together** the silver and gold fondant to make a marble pattern. Divide it into 12 equal-size balls, about 2 teaspoons each, and roll each into a rope, bend it in half, and twist and pinch the ends to form a horn.

NATURE MAGIC

**4. Top a cupcake** with a swirl of frosting from the piping bag. (It's best to frost and decorate one cupcake at a time.) Attach two marshmallow ears and a fondant horn. Scatter with sprinkles. Frost and decorate the remaining cupcakes.

Nature Magic 105

# Fairy House

You can build fairy houses with just a handful of whimsical candies, like rainbow sour tape for a sweet, colorful roof, and flower sprinkles for a garden of dainty blossoms.

**Here's What You Need**

- 12 cupcakes
- 2 cups white frosting
- Green food coloring
- Piping bag fitted with a grass tip
- 4 chocolate peanut butter wafer cookies
- 6 strips rainbow sour tape
- 12 mini white mints
- 6 gumdrops (any color)
- 12 nonpareil sprinkles
- Flower and butterfly sprinkles

**1. Set aside** ¼ cup of the frosting. In a medium bowl, tint the remaining frosting with the food coloring. Put the tinted frosting in the piping bag.

**2. Trim each wafer cookie** into 2-inch pieces, then trim one end of each piece into a point. Cut the sour tape into 1½-inch-long strips. Attach two strips of sour tape to the pointy end of each wafer cookie house using frosting and a toothpick. Use more frosting to add a mint chimney to each.

**3. Roll out each gumdrop** and trim it into two small doors. Attach one to each fairy house with a bit of the white frosting. Attach a nonpareil sprinkle doorknob with frosting to each door.

**4. Top a cupcake** with green frosting grass. (It's best to frost and decorate one cupcake at a time.) Press a fairy house in place, then scatter with flower sprinkles. Frost and decorate the remaining cupcakes.

Nature Magic 107

# The Gnome

Bring a little mythic charm to your birthday party with a platter of bearded gnome cupcakes. We held a cupcake design contest while making this book, asking kids to send us their ideas. This delightful design is based on one submitted by Madeline Keil, our grand-prize winner!

### Here's What You Need

- 12 cupcakes
- 2¼ cups white frosting
- Piping bag fitted with a star tip
- 3 tablespoons red sparkling sugar
- 12 cone-shaped corn snacks
- 12 brown or yellow mini jellybeans
- 24 mini brown, blue, or green chocolate gems

**1. Place 2 cups of the frosting** in the piping bag and place the sparkling sugar in a small bowl. Line a baking sheet with parchment paper. Use a mini spatula to cover the outside of a corn snack with some of the remaining frosting. Working over a bowl, sprinkle the snack generously with sugar, then place it on the prepared sheet. Repeat with the remaining corn snacks, frosting, and sugar.

**2. Working with one cupcake at a time,** pipe dollops of frosting around the edge of the cupcake for the hair and beard, as shown. Add a mustache.

Nature Magic

**3. Press a jellybean nose** into the frosting of the mustache.

**4. Use a toothpick** to add two dots of frosting to the face and attach the chocolate gem eyes. Press on a corn snack hat. Frost and decorate the remaining cupcakes.

Nature Magic  **109**

# Funny Faces

**Make someone smile with a funny face cupcake!**

With some frosting and sweet supplies, you can decorate cupcakes to look like emojis, aliens, or party friends.

# Kooky Emojis

Making a batch of these silly faces is a cinch! Start with bright yellow buttercream and learn a technique to form a flat top before you add edible facial features. Turn the page for some more ideas.

**Here's What You Need**

- 12 cupcakes
- 2 cups buttercream frosting
- Yellow food coloring
- Piping bags fitted with a round tip and a writing tip
- 2 to 3 strips red sour tape
- ½ cup chocolate or black frosting
- 12 candy eyes

**1. Line a baking sheet** with parchment paper. In a medium bowl, tint the buttercream frosting with the food coloring. Put the buttercream frosting in the piping bag with the round tip. Center the tip of the piping bag in the middle of a cupcake and, holding it in place, pipe out a ½-inch-thick dollop. Immediately turn the cupcake upside down on the parchment paper to create a flat top. Repeat with the remaining frosting and cupcakes. Put the baking sheet in the freezer for 15 minutes.

**Funny Faces**

**2.** **While you wait,** trim the sour tape into tongues. Put the chocolate frosting in the piping bag with the writing tip.

**3.** **Pipe a smiling mouth and eyes** on each cupcake. Add the tongues and candy eyes.

Funny Faces

# ENDLESS EMOJIS

With so many options, it's hard to choose which emojis to make in cupcake form. We picked a few, but feel free to use them for inspiration. Follow the method on page 112 for flattening the frosting before adding the decorations. We used yellow frosting for our designs but you can choose any color you wish!

### Cool Dude
Cutout Sunglasses (from the back of the book) + Piped Chocolate Frosting Smile

### Love Struck
Jumbo Heart Sprinkle Eyes + Piped Chocolate Frosting Smile

### LOL
Piped Chocolate Frosting Smile and Closed Eyes + Candy-Coated Sunflower Seed Tears

114  **Funny Faces**

### Oh, No!
**Piped Chocolate Frosting Mouth, Eyes, and Eyebrows +
Candy-Coated Sunflower Seed Tears**

### Kooky
**Piped Chocolate Frosting Smile and Closed Eye +
Candy Eye +
Red Sour Tape Tongue (page 112)**

### Smiley Face
**Piped Chocolate Frosting Smile and Eyes**

Funny Faces 115

# Zombie Faces

These zombie cupcakes are frighteningly easy to make with green frosting and minty teeth. Don't be afraid to eat two!

**Here's What You Need**

- 12 cupcakes
- 2 cups white frosting
- Green food coloring
- Black food coloring
- Piping bag fitted with a writing tip
- Black edible marker
- 24 round fruit candies (we used chewy fruit mints)
- 36 mini white mints
- 24 neon green banana candies
- Black sprinkles (optional)
- Pink pearl and nonpareil sprinkles (optional)

**1. In a small bowl,** tint 1½ cups of the frosting with the green food coloring. In a separate small bowl, tint the remaining frosting with the black food coloring. Put the black frosting in the piping bag.

**2. Use the edible marker** to draw pupils on each of the fruit candies to make eyes.

**3. Top a cupcake with an even layer** of the green frosting, about 2 tablespoons. (It's best to frost and decorate one cupcake at a time.) Press on two eyes.

116    Funny Faces

**4.** **Use the candies** to make silly, scary faces on the cupcakes. Pipe on scars and mouths with the black frosting.

# Oozing Aliens

These green cupcakes are out of this world. Melted green candy gives them their bloblike appearance.

**Here's What You Need**

- 12 cupcakes
- 1 cup green candy melts
- 4 teaspoons vegetable oil
- 2 cups white frosting
- Candy eyes
- Green pearl sprinkles
- Green nonpareils

**1. In a microwave-safe bowl,** combine the candy melts with the vegetable oil. Microwave the mixture for 1 minute. Stir it, then heat in 10-second bursts, stirring between each heating, until the candy is melted.

**2. Top each cupcake** with an even layer of frosting, about 2 tablespoons.

**3. Working with one cupcake** at a time, spoon some melted candy onto the top of the cupcake, creating a blob shape. If you like, use a toothpick to gently spread and smooth the surface of the candy. Immediately scatter candy eyes, sprinkles, and nonpareils onto the candy before it sets.

118  Funny Faces

**4. Decorate the remaining cupcakes.** If necessary, return the candy to the microwave for a few seconds to soften it.

# Cupcake Self-Portraits

At your next family gathering, neighborhood potluck, or classroom event, invite everyone to design their own cupcake self-portrait to celebrate your group. Set out frosting tinted in various skin tones and hair colors, with candies to match eyes.

**Here's What You Need**

- 12 cupcakes
- 4 cups frosting (2 cups each white and chocolate for eyes, skin, and hair tones or to suit your group)
- Food coloring for hair and skin tones
- Piping bag fitted with writing tip
- Piping bags fitted with round, star, and grass tips
- Black licorice lace
- Chocolate or fruit-flavored chews
- 12 heart sprinkles
- Blue, green, and brown chocolate gems

**1. Divide the frosting** into small bowls and tint each with the food coloring. Use 2 cups for various skin tones, 1½ cups for hair colors, and leave ½ cup white. Put the white frosting in the piping bag with the writing tip. Put each hair color in a piping bag with a different tip. Set out the licorice lace and candies for hair, heart sprinkles, and chocolate gems in separate bowls.

**2. Have each person** frost a cupcake to match their skin tone, then use the bagged frosting to pipe on a nose. Pipe dots of white frosting and press on chocolate gems for the eyes.

Funny Faces

**3. Add a fun hairstyle.** You can use more frosting piped with a star, round, or grass tip. Or attach candies for the hair. Add a heart sprinkle mouth.

Funny Faces  121

# Let's Celebrate!

**It's party time!** Whether you're hosting a birthday bash or celebrating a special holiday, you'll find super decorating ideas for your next gathering in this chapter.

# Friends 4 Ever!

Having BFFs over for a sleepover? Before bedtime, invite everyone to make their own friendship bracelet cupcake.

**Here's What You Need**

- 12 cupcakes
- 2 cups white frosting
- Food coloring, any color
- Black edible marker
- White chocolate gem candies
- Pearl sprinkles
- Shape sprinkles, such as hearts and stars

**1. In a medium bowl,** tint the frosting with the food coloring. (You can divide the frosting and make different colors, if you wish.) Use the edible marker to write each letter of your (or the recipient's) name on a chocolate gem candy.

**2. Have each guest** top a cupcake with an even layer of frosting, about 2 tablespoons. Arrange the lettered candies at the bottom of the cupcake to form your names, as shown. Use tweezers to add pearl and shaped sprinkles around the edge of the cupcake to form a bracelet.

Let's Celebrate! 125

# Bunch o' Balloons

Nothing says celebration quite like a balloon bouquet. The best part about these is that they won't float away!

**Here's What You Need**

- 12 cupcakes
- 2 cups white frosting
- Toothpick or skewer
- Food coloring
- Licorice lace
- 12 mini jellybeans (colors should match your frosting choice)

**1. Divide the frosting** into several small bowls. Tint each bowl of frosting a different color with food coloring. Cut the licorice lace into 4-inch lengths.

**2. Poke a hole** with a toothpick or skewer in the side of each cupcake.

**3. Top a cupcake** with an even layer of frosting, about 2 tablespoons. (It's best to frost and decorate one cupcake at a time.) Add a matching color jellybean to the cupcake, centered over the poked hole.

Let's Celebrate!

**4. Insert a licorice lace** balloon string into each hole below the jellybean. Frost and decorate the remaining cupcakes.

# Soccer Balls

Score big with your soccer teammates when you bring these to the next match. Use the stencil from the back of the book to ensure each ball is league approved!

**Here's What You Need**

- 12 cupcakes
- 2 cups buttercream frosting
- Piping bag fitted with a jumbo round tip
- ½ cup chocolate frosting
- Piping bag fitted with a writing tip
- Soccer ball template from the back of the book
- Toothpicks

**1. Line a baking sheet** with parchment paper. Put the buttercream frosting in the piping bag with the jumbo round tip. Center the tip of the piping bag in the middle of a cupcake and, holding it in place, pipe out a ½-inch-thick dollop. Immediately turn the cupcake upside down on the parchment paper to create a flat surface. Repeat with the remaining frosting and cupcakes. Put the baking sheet in the freezer for 15 minutes.

**2. Meanwhile,** put the chocolate frosting in the piping bag with the writing tip. Peel the parchment paper off the chilled cupcakes.

Let's Celebrate!

**3.** **Place the soccer ball template** on a cupcake. Use a toothpick to score lines in the frosting, following the template. Carefully remove the template.

**4.** **Following the toothpick lines,** pipe on lines of the chocolate frosting to make the cupcake look like a soccer ball. Fill in a few of the shapes.

**5.** **Decorate** the remaining cupcakes.

Let's Celebrate!   **129**

# GO TEAM!

There will be high fives all around for these team-themed treats. Follow the directions for the soccer ball on the previous pages to flatten the frosting surface of any design before you start decorating.

## We're #1!
Star or Round Tip Frosting Dollop **+** Toothpick **+** Number 1 Sticker (from the back of the book)

## Soccer Ball
White Frosting **+** Chocolate Frosting Pattern (page 128)

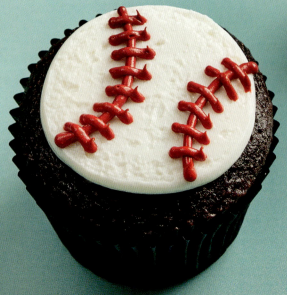

## Baseball
White Frosting **+** Red Frosting Stitching

130   Let's Celebrate!

## Basketball
Orange Frosting +
Chocolate Frosting Lines

## Tennis Ball
Yellow Frosting +
White Frosting Lines

Let's Celebrate! **131**

# Conversation Hearts

On Valentine's Day, give out heart-shaped cupcakes with thoughtful frosting messages. The trick for shaping them into hearts is simply a little ball of foil.

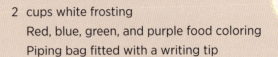

**Here's What You Need**

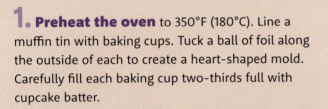

Baking cups
Aluminum foil rolled into 12 (½-inch) balls
Batter for 12 cupcakes (see recipe on page 16)

2 cups white frosting
Red, blue, green, and purple food coloring
Piping bag fitted with a writing tip

**1. Preheat the oven** to 350°F (180°C). Line a muffin tin with baking cups. Tuck a ball of foil along the outside of each to create a heart-shaped mold. Carefully fill each baking cup two-thirds full with cupcake batter.

**2. Bake for 20 minutes,** or until a toothpick inserted in the center of a cupcake comes out clean. Let cool completely.

**3. In a medium bowl,** tint ⅓ cup of the frosting red and place it in the piping bag. Evenly divide the remaining frosting into four small bowls, and tint each with a different hue of food coloring.

**4. Top a cupcake** with an even layer of colored frosting, about 2 tablespoons. Use the the red frosting to pipe Valentine messages, such as Be Mine, Sweet, XOXO, Bestie, and so on.

**5. Frost and decorate** the remaining cupcakes.

# Piñata Party

Just like their crepe paper counterparts, these colorful goodies are filled with a surprise, but instead of smashing them, you take a bite!

**Here's What You Need**

- 12 cupcakes
- 2 cups frosting
  Blue, orange, yellow, and magenta food coloring
- 4 piping bags fitted with writing tips
- Apple corer
- ¼ cup mini chocolate pastels or other small candies or sprinkles

**1. Evenly divide the frosting** among four bowls and tint each a different color with the food coloring. Put each color of frosting in a separate piping bag.

**2. Cut a hole in the center** of each cupcake with an apple corer, taking care not to go all the way down to the bottom. Reserve the cake pieces.

**3. Fill the hole in each cupcake** with mini candies and sprinkles, then top with a reserved cake piece. (You may need to trim the bottom of each piece so it sits evenly on top of the cupcake.)

**4. Starting at the bottom of a cupcake,** pipe a zigzag line of frosting across the surface to make a layer of "streamers." Repeat with the remaining colors, overlapping each layer slightly as you move up. Frost the remaining cupcakes.

Let's Celebrate!

Let's Celebrate!

# Pumpkin Patch

In addition to carving pumpkins for Halloween, bake up a batch of cupcakes to decorate. You can assemble your jack-o'-lanterns to look like the ones pictured or design your own silly or scary faces.

**Here's What You Need**

- 12 cupcakes
- 12 chocolate chews
- 2 cups white frosting
- Red and yellow food coloring
- 12 green mini mints

**1. Knead each chocolate chew** with your fingers, then roll it out. Use kitchen scissors or mini food cutters to trim them into parts for 12 pumpkin faces.

**2. In a medium bowl,** tint the white frosting with red and yellow food coloring, making orange. Top a cupcake with an even layer of frosting, about 2 tablespoons. Use a mini offset spatula to sweep across the cupcake from top to bottom to form ridges on the cupcake's surface.

Let's Celebrate!

**3. Rotate the cupcake**
so the bottom is now the top.

**4. Add a green mint stem**
and a chocolate chew face.
Frost and decorate the remaining cupcakes.

Let's Celebrate!     **137**

# Candy-Colored Christmas Trees

Looking for a festive idea for a holiday party? Melt green candies to make trees, then top them with candy sprinkles and stars for ornaments.

**Here's What You Need**

- 12 cupcakes
- 1 cup (about 6 ounces) green candy melts
- Piping bag fitted with a writing tip
- Christmas tree template (page 144)
- 12 pretzel sticks
- Nonpareil sprinkle mix
- 12 jumbo star sprinkles
- ½ cup shredded coconut
- 2 cups white frosting

**1. Put the candy melts** in a microwave-safe bowl and heat on high power for 1 minute. Stir vigorously. Continue to microwave in 10-second bursts, stirring thoroughly after each, until the candy is melted. Put the melted candy in the piping bag.

**2. Cut out the Christmas tree template** from the back of the book. Lay a piece of parchment paper over it. Center a pretzel stick over the outline, letting the end of the pretzel hang past the edge of the tree shape to form the trunk.

**3. Pipe zigzag lines of candy** over the pretzel stick, following the outlines to form a Christmas tree. Immediately scatter on nonpareil sprinkle mix and add a star sprinkle to the top. Repeat with the remaining pretzels, candy, and sprinkles. Let the candy trees set at room temperature until firm.

**138**  Let's Celebrate!

# MERRY CHRISTMAS

**4. Put the coconut** in a shallow bowl. Top a cupcake with an even layer of white frosting (about 2 tablespoons), then dip it in the coconut to coat. (It's best to frost and decorate one cupcake at a time.) Add a pretzel stick tree by inserting its trunk into the cupcake. Frost and decorate the remaining cupcakes.

# Index

## A
aliens, 118–19
animals, 50–67. *See also* bugs; fish; snakes

## B
baking, 10–13, 18
balloons, 126–27
balls, 128–31
birthdays, 46–47
boats, 70–71
bugs, 98–101
buttercream frosting, 20–21

## C
candy, 14, 30–33, 38. *See also* marshmallows; sprinkles
　Christmas Trees, 138–39, 144
　-filled cupcakes, 134–35
　geodes, 88–89
　melts, 30
　molds, 12–13, 31
cats, 56–57
celebration cupcakes, 122–39. *See also* birthdays; holidays
chocolate. *See also* candy
　cupcake recipe, 18–19
　frosting recipe, 21
Christmas trees, 122, 138–39, 144
clouds, 48–49
color mixing, 24–25
cookies, 14–15, 33, 42–43, 80–81
conversation hearts, 132–33
cupcakes
　recipes, 16–19
　uses for, 9

## D
decorating basics, 23–35
　dots, 44–45
　marshmallow clouds, 48–49
　rainbows, 48–49
　sprinkles, 38–43
　squiggles, 44–45
decorations, stocking up on, 14–15
dinosaurs, 66–67
dogs, 52–55
dots, 44–45

## E
Earth, 84–85, 87
emojis, 112–15
equipment, 12–14, 27–29, 31–34
equivalents and conversions, 11

## F
faces, 110–21
fairy houses, 106–7
fish, 72–77
　shark fin templates, 143
flowers, 94–97
fondant, 14, 34–35
food coloring, 24–25
friendship bracelets, 124–25
frogs, 64–65
frosting, 20–21, 24, 29

## G
geodes, 88–89
gnomes, 108–9
graham cracker sand, 33
grass piping tip, 29, 52–53

## H
Halloween, 136–37
heart-shaped cupcakes, 132–33
holidays, 84–85, 132–33, 136–39, 144
houses, fairy, 106–7

## I
invitations, 142

## J
jimmies. *See* sprinkles

## L
lions, 51, 62–63

## M
magical creatures, 78–79, 104–5, 108–9. *See also* fairy houses
map, treasure, 82–83
marshmallows, 14, 33, 48–49
melting candy, 30–31
mermaid, 78–79
metric conversions, 11
molds for candy, 12–13, 31
moon, 87

## N
nature-themed cupcakes, 92–109
numbers, 46–47

## P
panda bears, 50, 58–59
paw prints, 54
piñata, 134–35
piping bag and tips, 12, 27–29
　grass piping tip, 52–53
　round piping tip, 46–47
　star piping tip, 46–47
　writing piping tip, 44–45
pirate map, 82–83
planets, 84–87
pretzels, 13
pumpkins, 136–37
puppies, 54–55

## R
rainbows, 48–49
recipes
　cupcakes, 16–19
　frosting, 20–21
rockets, 90–91
rope, fondant, 35
round piping tip, 29, 46–47

## S
safety tips, 18, 20, 30, 32
sandcastles, 80–81
sea-themed cupcakes, 68–83
shark fins, 76–77, 143
sloths, 60–61
snakes, 102–3
sour tape, 14, 33
spiders, 101
sports, 128–31
sprinkles, 38–43
squiggles, 44–45
star piping tip, 29, 46–47
stars, 86
stencils, 40–41, 142–44
stickers, 142
storing cupcakes, 11
sugar for decorating, 38–41
sun, 87
supplies, 14–15

**T**

templates, 142
tinting frosting, 24–25
tips. *See also* piping bags and tips
    decorating, 23
    safety, 18, 20, 30, 32
    using fondant, 34
tools, 12–14, 27–29, 31–34
treasure map, 82–83
twisted rope, fondant, 35

**U**

unicorns, 104–5

**V**

Valentine's Day, 132–33
vanilla
    buttercream, 20–21
    cupcakes, 16–17

**W**

words
    conversation hearts, 132–33
    friendship bracelets, 124–25
    hip, hip, hooray cupcakes, 42–43
    writing piping tip and, 29
worms, 101
writing piping tip, 29, 44–45

**Z**

zombies, 116–17

# Cupcake Designs by Chapter

**CHAPTER 3:**
## Sprinkles, Dots & Squiggles

All about Sprinkles 38–39
Sugar Stenciled 40–41
Hip, Hip, Hooray! 42–43
Squiggles & Dots 44–45
Number 8 Cake 46–47
Rainbows & Marshmallow Clouds 48–49

**CHAPTER 4:**
## Animals, Animals Everywhere!

Goodie Golden Retriever 52–53
A Pack of Pup Cakes! 54–55
Calico Kitty 56–57
Candy Panda 58–59
Choc-o-Sloth 60–61
Roaring Lion 62–63
Frog on a Log 64–65
Gumdrop Dinosaur 66–67

**CHAPTER 5:**
## Sea & Stars

Sail Away! 70–71
School of Cool 72–73
Rainbow Jellyfish 74–75
Shark Fins 76–77
Dreamy Mermaid Tails 78–79
Cookie Sandcastles 80–81
Pirate Map of Treasures 82–83
Planet Earth 84–85
Awesome Planets 86–87
Hard Candy Geodes 88–89
Mini Cone Rockets 90–91

**CHAPTER 6:**
## Nature Magic

Daisy Cakes 94–95
Flower Garden 96–97
Ant Attack 98–99
Creepy Crawlers 100–1
Slithering Snakes 102–3
Mystical Unicorns 104–5
Fairy House 106–7
The Gnome 108–9

**CHAPTER 7:**
## Funny Faces

Kooky Emojis 112–13
Endless Emojis 114–15
Zombie Faces 116–17
Oozing Aliens 118–19
Cupcake Self-Portraits 120–21

**CHAPTER 8:**
## Let's Celebrate!

Friends 4 Ever! 124–25
Bunch o' Balloons 126–27
Soccer Balls 128–29
Go Team! 130–31
Conversation Hearts 132–33
Piñata Party 134–35
Pumpkin Patch 136–37
Candy-Colored Christmas Trees 138–39

# Cupcake Extras

On the following pages, you'll find stickers, templates, stencils, and cupcake toppers.

**Templates:** Cut out the shark fin and Christmas tree template page. Cover the templates with a piece of parchment paper and use them as a guideline for making melted candy shapes.

**Stickers:** Fold the stickers in half over toothpicks to make decorative cupcake toppers.

**Stencils:** Separate the stencils along the perforated lines and place on the cupcake. Use them to make patterns of colored sugar and sprinkles (see page 40 for directions), or the soccer ball on page 128.

**Toppers:** Carefully tear out the palm trees and the sunglasses. Place them onto the frosting to serve (and remove to eat!).

**Cupcake Party Invitations:** Fill out and send these to friends to get them excited about your party. If you need extras, photocopy them.

# Shark Fin Template, page 76

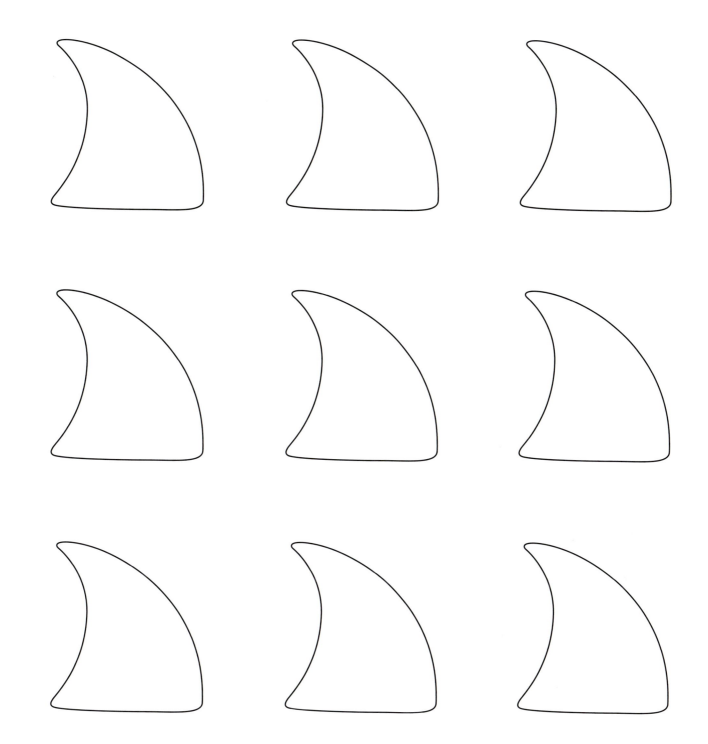

# Christmas Tree Template, page 138

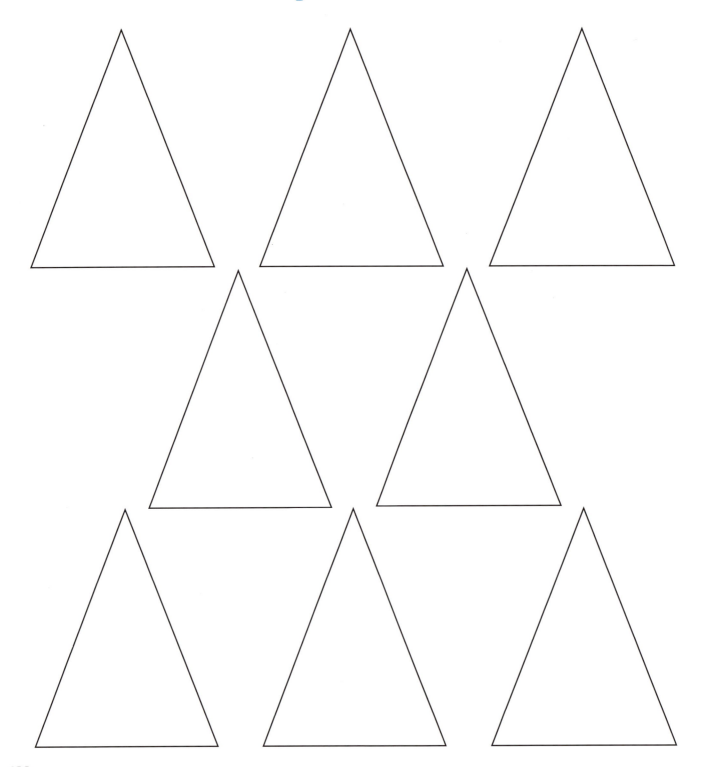

# Cupcake Stickers

# Sailboat Stickers, page 70